The Woman, the Mink, the Cod and the Donkey

SPHERE

First published in Great Britain in 2021 by Sphere

5 7 9 10 8 6

Copyright © Little, Brown Book Group 2021
Illustrations by Emanuel Santos

A CIP catalogue record for this book
is available from the British Library.

ISBN 978-0-7515-8431-8

Printed and bound in Great Britain by Clays Ltd, Elcograf S.p.A.

Papers used by Sphere are from well-managed forests
and other responsible sources.

Sphere
An imprint of
Little, Brown Book Group
Carmelite House
50 Victoria Embankment
London EC4Y 0DZ

An Hachette UK Company
www.hachette.co.uk

www.littlebrown.co.uk

The Woman, the Mink, the Cod and the Donkey

(An affectionate parody)

Text by Margerie Swash

Illustrations by Emanuel Santos

Welcome to my book. It's warm and safe in here, which you will have guessed already because it's about a human and three animals. You might not be able to remember the animals or the order they fall within the title, but that doesn't matter. The pictures will remind you that my story is about a woman, a mink, a ~~salmon~~ cod and a donkey. Let me tell you a bit more about them.

The woman is embarking on an important journey. She does not know her destination, but she knows what she'll find when she gets there: an open pub. It has been a long time since she has been in one due to a strange, sad region of yesteryear called 'Lockdown'.

On her travels she finds a mink. The mink is wise because he's known the cruelties of life, having been maligned because Danish minks were found to be spreading Coronavirus.

The woman helps the mink forget the cruelties of life through something as old as

time itself: love. The mink
helps the woman withstand
the journey to the pub
through something else as
old as time itself: wine.

As they wander on
their quest, they meet a
cod. It will never be easy
for a mink to meet a
cod because cod is tasty to
mink. Cod is also tasty to
non-vegetarian/vegan women, but not on this
occasion because it's still swimming around,
and it's not covered in batter. (You might
be wondering how the cod travels with the
woman and the mink. Don't worry, it'll
make sense when you get to that part in the
book.) At the beginning of the story, the cod
is afraid, because its species has been
over-fished.

Finally, they meet a donkey. (No, it's not
Eeyore — this isn't 'Winnie the Pooh'.) The

donkey is the noisiest thing they've ever met,
yet never has anything useful or interesting
to say. The irony. We all know a donkey.

***

I'm writing this book in a time when things
aren't very funny and no pubs are open, in
the hope that by the time you read this, pubs
will be open again and therefore you'll
be more likely to find any-and everything
funny, including this book. I hope you're
reading it in a time when three animals for
company seems sweet, and not a necessity

because of social distancing. But whenever
you're reading it, I hope it makes you smile.
If all else fails, go buy yourself a balloon.
As the woman says, after the mink has given
her a balloon:

'Nobody can be uncheered with a balloon.'*
*Quote by A. A. Milne, 'Winnie the Pooh'

'Hello'

'What are you looking for?'
asked the mink.

'An open door,'
said the woman.

'Because people shut you out?'
asked the mink.

'No, literally
an open door;
all the pubs are
closed.'

'I'm lonely, can I look with you?' asked the mink.

'I'm sober, yet I'm talking to a... ferret? Otter?'

'Sure,' said the woman.

'Which way shall we go?'
    asked the woman.

'It doesn't matter, so long as
I'm with you,' said the mink.

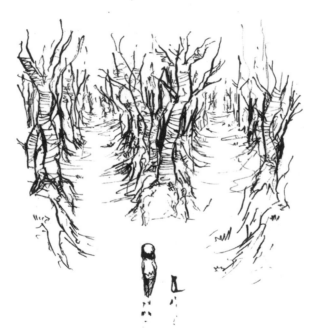

'. . . But seriously, which way
        shall we go?'

'Would you rather be famous
or rich?' asked the woman.

'I'd rather be kind,'
said the mink.

'Yes, we
all want
to be kind,
but that's
not how
the game
works.'

'. . . Rich, then.'

'Why are you looking for a pub?' asked the mink.

'I really like wine,'
said the woman.

'Why are you lonely?'
asked the woman.

'People don't like minks
much,' said the mink.

'That's not very nice,'
said the woman.

'Well, they think we carry
disease,' said the mink.

'So now you don't need to find a pub, do you?' said the mink.

'I can't work out what it is,' said the woman, 'but something's missing. Let's carry on looking.'

'Maybe,' said the mink,
'the pubs aren't open
because it's only 10 in the
morning. What about going
somewhere where it's . . . .
10 in the evening?!'

'You are the cleverest mink in the world,' said the woman.

'What did you learn from the rainstorm?' asked the woman.

'That the sun always comes out again,' said the mink. '...And the sheer mechanical brilliance of umbrellas. You?'

'Definitely the umbrella thing.'

'Hi there,' said the woman.

'Where are you going in such a hurry?' asked the mink.

'An owl and a pussycat in a boat were chasing me with a net,' said the cod.

'An owl and a pussycat.
Someone's been at sea
too long, methinks.'

'Isn't it funny that
sometimes we think
we're running away from
something — but in the
end, we're always running
towards something,'
said the mink.

'What do you think we should do differently in the future?' asked the mink.

'Stop allowing politicians and the media to portray refugees as criminals,' said the cod.

'. . . . I was going to say
we should spend less time
on social media,'
said the woman.

'Both very good suggestions,' said the mink.

'Do you ever get cross?'
    asked the mink.

'All the time,'
    said the woman.

'How do you let go?'
    asked the mink.

'I make mashed potato.'

'Do you ever feel sad?'
asked the mink.

'Oh yes,'
said the woman.

'What do you do
to feel better?'

'I make mashed
potato with cheese.'

'Where are you
sailing to?'
asked the cod.

'Australia,' said the woman.
'We've come from the
morning, where the pubs
are closed. It's the evening
over there, so the pubs will be
open,' said the mink.

we

Are

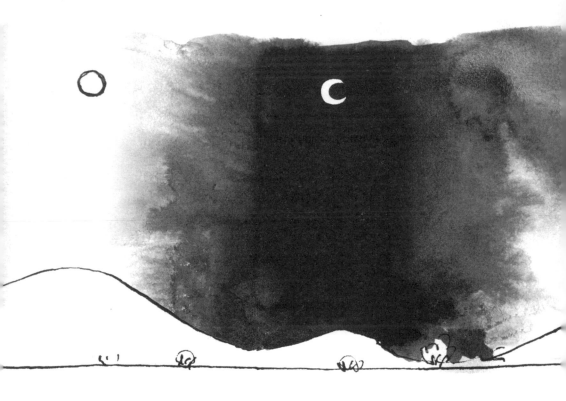

these

yet?

Would you rather travel through time or turn invisible whenever you feel like it?

Are you famous?

I went to the market and I bought an apple, a ball ...

I spy
with my
little eye,
something
beginning
with W...

Are you
an actress?

Are you a singer?

'I'm beginning to think the person who said "It's about the journey, not the destination" never went on a journey,' said the woman.

'I wish I could come with you,' said the cod.

'You could come in this?' suggested the woman.

'I can't do that,' said the cod.
'Surely you need your glass?'

'You're more important,'
said the woman.

'(Plus, this is a gin glass
and I'm on the wine
at the moment.)'

'The nearest pub is ages away,' said the mink. 'How will we get these?'

'Hello.'

'Hee-haw, hee-
haw, bleach,
hee-haw,
hee-haw,'
said the
donkey.

'Would you mind giving us a ride to the nearest pub?' asked the woman.

'Hee-haw, hee-
haw, sense,
hee-haw,
hee-haw,'
said the
donkey.

'What's the most valuable
lesson you've learned in
your life so far?'
said the woman.

'Start paying into your pension early,' said the mink.

'Always take out travel insurance,' said the cod.

'Hee-haw, hee-haw, postal votes, hee-haw,' said the donkey.

'What about you?' asked the mink.

'Only wear knickers with a breathable gusset,' said the woman.

'Hi—' the mink started to say.

'Shh,' said the woman. 'Three animals is quite enough.'

'Look, an open pub!'
said the cod.

'This isn't the one,' said the
woman. 'Let's keep looking.'

lee-haw   hee-haw   lee-haw

                   hee-haw   hee-haw

'Hee-haw,
                                        hee-haw
    hee-haw,
                                  hee-haw

hee-haw
              hee-haw'

        hee-haw

hee-haw

said the donkey.

'It is a good lesson,'
said the mink.

'What is?' asked
the woman.

'That there's no mute
button in life.'

'Look, another open pub!'
said the cod.

'This isn't the one,' said the
woman. 'Let's keep looking.'

'I wish I had a smaller nose.'

'I wish I had a bigger tail.'

'Hee-haw, hee-haw toupée, hee-haw.'

'I wish I had less oily skin.'

'I didn't think once about what I looked like when we were in the boat,' said the woman.

'Are you thinking what I'm thinking?' said the mink.

'Yes,' said the cod. 'We need to work on self-lo—'

'That works too,'
said the woman.

'Look, yet another
open pub!' said the cod.

'It wasn't an open pub I was looking for,' said the woman. 'It was an open pub with strangers happy all around me; with my friends next to me — that's what I was looking for.'

The

End